Came the Lightening

TWENTY POEMS FOR GEORGE

OLIVIA HARRISON

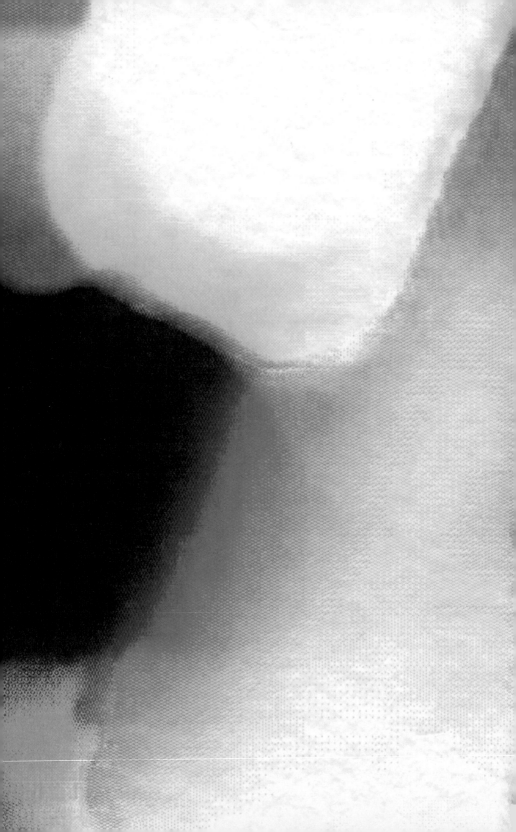

Came the Lightening

TWENTY POEMS FOR GEORGE

OLIVIA HARRISON

Genesis Publications

First published in 2022 by
Genesis Publications Ltd

ISBN: 978-1-905662-73-9

Printed and bound in Italy
by Grafiche Milani

1 3 5 7 9 10 8 6 4 2

This book first appeared
as a limited edition of
1,500 numbered copies,
signed by Olivia Harrison

Genesis Publications Ltd
Genesis House
2 Jenner Road, Guildford
Surrey, England, GU1 3PL

Fine Books and Prints Since 1974
w genesis-publications.com

To George for lighting the fire

To Dhani for fuelling it.

Where are you, where have you gone?
There's nothing left of your bonfires
but drifting dust
And, on our hands, burn marks
Or the imprint of flowers.
In the end I've found you
On the blank page in front of me.

Pablo Neruda, 'Oda al fuego', *Odas Elementales*

CONTENTS

FOREWORD

I'm writing these words of introduction to this very special book in the spirit of friendship. During the years we spent making *Living in the Material World*, Olivia Harrison became a close, treasured friend, and for that I feel blessed.

I'm also writing in the spirit of admiration.

How could Olivia give form to her memories of a life shared with her beloved George Harrison, now gone twenty years? She might have done an oral history or a memoir.

Instead, she composed a work of poetic autobiography.

Poetry can move through time and space. It can shift scale from the microscopic to the infinite and back again with just a word, and the cosmos can be felt in the smallest thing. Throughout the work, Olivia evokes the most fleeting gestures and instants, plucked from the flow of time and memory and *felt* through her choice of words and the overall rhythm.

In this suite of twenty poems, Olivia gives us the movement of her life, from childhood on to the love that she and George found together, a love that they nurtured and allowed to grow and flourish into pure acceptance. Acceptance of beauty, of mutual respect and affection... acceptance of the gift of their son, Dhani... acceptance of change and shock and violence... acceptance of death and loss and transformation.

The poems are grounded in the sustaining power of the earth, in the gardens and groves and lawns and wild places that George and Olivia tended so carefully throughout their cherished Friar Park. They tended and they watched and listened, to the earth, its movements and metamorphoses. 'I lost track of time and, finally, I lost track of grief. / Death is good for the garden.'

This is a work that celebrates love but sees its transitory nature with clarity. This is a lament for a loved one gone and a clear-eyed recognition that sadness is fleeting. And this is a work that embraces impermanence. 'No footsteps taken backwards, just the hill that I'll descend,' writes Olivia in the final poem, 'Townsfolk will tell stories and mourn our era's end.'

I wish that everyone were fortunate enough to have a friend like Olivia Harrison. This book of poems offers an imprint of her generous spirit.

MARTIN SCORSESE

I

ANOTHER SPRING

All I wanted was another spring. Was it so much to ask?
I thought it might be granted and we would see another April day,
That we would warm by each other's side and our faces
Would abide by the denier's rule and muffle our cries,
The corners of our lips upturned towards the sky
But not enough to mask the cruelty of birth and death,
Pulling our fingers from each other's tips,
Scanning our swirling prints to remember the smallest whorls and
Loops, your palm of stars, in this final parting at too early an hour.
The winter wouldn't come and time just stalled,
Then the four winds turned on us, whistling...
... *that is all, that is all, that is all.*

On that final day, I cleansed myself with water and air
To be devoid of earthly residues that may have held you here:
My scent or whimper, the smell of my hair.
I wanted you to leave without any impediments of care
To float away like you always imagined and prepared.
I couldn't help myself and nuzzled your ear
And whispered final words to leave you with my sound
As a signpost to my soul, wherever we are bound,
The formless state of nothingness where emotions are consumed
For now, alone in winter feeling spring will never bloom.

December 2001

II

TUUM CORPUS

I was graced by the touch of his elegant hands,
Exact and delicate, but strong like a man's
Pruning a bonsai, on the wheel in a race,
Finding jade in the sand or touching my face.
A small mole above his wrist sat in a nest of fine hair
And another mark he and I knew was there:
A faint scar across four fingers slashed by fish scales
As he threw the dead minnow back onto the reef,
Just a shimmer of silver, he looked so big in the mask.
Instant karma, he said, for a frivolous act.

Girlish long torso with narrow hips shaped by rations of war
Only filling out after thirty years or more.
Renowned for his explosion of rebellious dark hair
Veiling finely tuned treasures of sticky-out ears
Standing alert at attention, Venus flytraps
Stalking innocent notes to find their place on the staff
Proposing to words he hadn't known long
His newlywed verses, down the aisle with a song.

Blazing eyes were not empty or vague, didn't flitter
Focused and angry they could silence a room
So intense, neither woman nor man was safe from a swoon
In distant stare I knew he could see
Through something that made him reluctant to be
Tied to the story of this impermanent place,
Impatient to plant the bigger landscape.

As his life slowed and rolled to a halt
His eyes moved in tandem to the world at his feet,
Not locked straight ahead or down as in sleep.
Then up out of the world they turned
To the pinpoint of existence, no journey at all
Towards the prearranged rendezvous to wait for the call
When his trillions of atoms could leave their formation
The force of a nova that shook seven gates
One eternal exhale, half a billion intakes.

III

END OF THE LINE

There is nothing like seeing the end of the path
In a one-point perspective, without right or left.
No shuffling of feet or stalling for time,
The stream of the Ganges left me behind.

We were so young, there were hours to spare
How could we imagine you not being there?
After a lifetime, Orpheus looked back
Then came the twist in the proverbial last act.

How were we as parents? I think we did right.
'How will you manage?' you asked me that night.
Were we examples of love and respect,
Leave a trail to the lofty, conceal our regrets?

Were you a good husband? Was I a good wife?
We forgot why we felt that we needed amends.
It seemed that we should, but we couldn't recall
All things that once hurt now irrelevant, small.

Remember that party when I went home alone?
In the mix, we ended up in two different plays.
The lines made no sense, so I cried and assumed,
Hailed a white taxi and stomped to my room.

When we pushed each other past our beyonds,
Drifting back and forth into arms,
Always finding ourselves deep once again
In the curves and shallows of each other's skin.

Like a song we managed to write all our lines,
Sang our duet, keeping pretty good time
In the right tempo, a couple false starts
With a chorus repeated by our beating hearts.
Our encore surrendered, we had to let go
We may do it all over, you just never know.

IV

MY ARRIVAL

In John and Yoko's long white car, eccentric in its fate,
Blacked-out windows, Persian rugs, we paused at wrought-iron gates.
From the town hall we heard Christmas carols, sung by a schoolboy choir,
Music for this middle-earth, a lush and loamy Shire.

Rolling up the drive, it was late and somehow seemed
The arboretum stood awaiting as a welcome meant for me.
A tiny gatehouse was so pretty, adorned by the village crest;
Three symbols carved in stone, a trinity to bless.

Was it stately home or cottage? Dark and fog were playing,
On cue a canine trio began a comic alto baying.
Two towering blue cedars sanctioned my arrival,
Arboreal first impressions, in true Victorian style.

With a sense of benediction, I mumbled secret words,
Nodding as we walked inside, thinking I'd overheard
Their branches waving judgement and like Alice I felt small,
Straining to read the verse carved high in the entry hall.

Something about a friend and a microscopic glass
Knowing all his faults, letting his foibles pass.
The room was dim, it echoed, the grandfather clock stood firm,
Its pendulum marked the moment, my cheeks began to burn.

Hurrying by to open one of the inner doors,
A hand now on my lower back, to move me slowly forward.
He felt my apprehension as the marble helped me glide
Onto the parquet floor, across the threshold like a bride.

Holly branches tied and hung, swags of tartan ribbon,
The fire throwing burning sparks, each one a flying vision
That awakened distant memories, brought forward to the now,
A clash of lives before us, with nothing disavowed.

Dwarfed beneath the chandelier, the polished oak and brass,
Details of that period, typically unabashed,
It felt eerily familiar as I sat there on my own,
Touched by his formality: 'Olivia, welcome home.'

My naivety was novel and bared so naturally,
Unadorned and unimpressed, as much a curiosity
As that famous mystery man living on the hill,
Never looking back, his purpose to fulfil.

Devoid of inhibitions in the California waves
I tried to place some flowers on the mantel, not a grave.
How was I to know that the English had such rules?
You had to earn that privilege, to me it was a ruse

To exorcise the dull and grey; it wasn't really fair
To expect a bunch of roses to change the atmosphere,
Illuminate the winter mood and scenes in leaded glass,
Dispel unspoken remnants of a recent broken past.

Unaware I'd missed the drama, so peaceful and serene
From the palette of a sunny beach to a hundred shades of green,
Until I got my bearings, I walked a little softly,
Replaced a sombre Turner with a bright blue Hockney.

By the Butterflies I was shunned, which somehow made me special,
Aspiring pretty girls with schemes that had potential
To charm the quiet one, a superficial prize,
In formidable deep currents, they skimmed but did not dive.

Musicians checking in and out, creating works of art,
A mournful tenor, dressed in black, put Lonely on the charts,
The southern gent with 'gator drawl, Americana in his stride,
The poet of a million words, elusive though not shy.

Two siblings set the standard born singing perfect parts,
Tones you couldn't separate, Little Susie, broken hearts,
The Rockabilly Cat, suede shoes outside his door,
Bopped the blues with Jerry Lee and rocked Sun Records Four.

With his hollow-bodied Gibson, Scotty rode that Mystery Train,
The famous Memphis solo every picker tries to tame.
One night the gang all gathered, asked how he did that thang?
The maestro plucked the air and said, 'Just grabbed a bunch of strings.'

The legendary Slowhand dropped in with the ex-Mrs,
He gave me some advice and two friendly welcome kisses,
Bare shoulder, Biba T-shirt, blonde hair on top her head;
I hung their apprehension, and overcoats of dread.

Two ladies of one house, always a little awkward.
The guys plugged in the Fender amps and blasted Robert Johnson;
With trembling lips she shed a tear, backlit by Gallé lamp,
Like an old Hollywood movie, gone with that last chance.

Single notes sustaining, feeling more like brothers,
Trying to get inside the clockwork of each other,
Riffing about their escapades, with much more interest in
12-bar blues and skiffle, than the mayhem trailing them.

Both young lead guitars traded licks as well as women
Female guile at play and damaging decisions.
Which way they would go, like trading cards, so sadly
Predictable exchanges and yes, they ended badly.

The triangle now a legend, grows as it lives on,
Appeared to be three-sided, was more a hexagon.
What felt like fun and freedom in a smoke haze of confusion
Were momentary fireworks in a decade of amusement.

Their lives no longer simple, preceded by their names,
Around the kitchen table, not a trace of fame,
In a language of their own, telepathic understanding
Maybe a little weary from what the muses were demanding.

Time inside the studio was surrendered as recluse;
I lost him to Apollo, Calliope and Zeus.
Winter took its toll, willingly inflicted;
The exhausted artist was bestowed with songs he knew were gifted.

Conquered by the equinox, early in the year,
Darkness bowed to longer days, he finally reappeared
With the hardiest of seedlings, no longer underground,
The victory of the chlorophyll that coloured winter's brown.

In the overgrowth of woodland he began a masterwork
As his hands became familiar with the coolness of the earth.
Solace came from rising shoots, organic and alive
Though intuition told him, he may not see them thrive.

Working with a fervour, counting down the days,
Camouflaged in khaki, boot with knotted lace,
He laid a serpentine of bark that led to his retreat.
I cried near the Sequoia, which became my weeping tree.

Like the tangle of roots that sustain yet are unseen,
His legacy surrounds me, in the planting and the singing.
I watched him shape the canopy, cut windows to the sky
Saw sunlight falling perfectly on the goodness of his life.

V

HER OR ME

Three words of love, a kiss on the head
A hint of your smile, so easily led
By diminished chords and open-tuned strings
Sanskrit mantras, Om Hreem Kleem.

My nervous whistle became the first note
Soon to be known as a song that he wrote
Add the flick of a butter knife ringing a glass
Cut crystal rhythms and spoon castanets.

A silent guitar, sometimes ignored
Then caressed and strummed
He fell in love once more.
Round and curvaceous like a woman, you see,
I wondered if he loved her much more than me.

VI

SOUTH

We caressed in a thermal haze of the south-facing wall where the sun god threw his fire
Anointing our tall shadows in the light of the longest day,
On whitewashed bricks that held heat of solar rays.
Saturn peaches soft to the touch, left squishy hollows where our fingers brushed,
Pricked by wild blackberries that stained our teeth and tongues.
Solstice brought its magic and a bunch of red grapes hung
Over the doorway, still bitter as the earth began to tilt,
Then juicy and dark before we surrendered to the fall
And headed for lower latitudes to watch fronds unfurl and Humpbacks call
Us to the very edge of the cliff where I stand now,
Wondering if I should drift down onto the rocks and dark sea,
To join the sirens in a surprising tragedy
Or wait for another sunrise on my face.
I hear you say surely that is a better place
To walk barefoot and pick ice blue calatheas,
Pink gingers, heliconias as a winter panacea.
Fleeting flavours traded on sticky lips betrayed by a harvest moon,
A rush to ripen early meant falling far too soon.
The price of summer love, a mirage of golden days
Came requital for the endless warmth, an exchange we had to pay.

VII

SONG FOR THE SON

A triad of lives ago I asked the father to write about the son.
At the passing of a word cloud, he began to softly hum
An ode to the child who arrived that stormy August night,
Three crops of wild black hair huddled into one, my indescribable delight.

Our shoulders sloped in humble bow, this blessing seemed so late
In hindsight, we had just embarked, still on our first date.
We were two, but always felt like three
Our initials fell so naturally, G, O and D.

Maiden to mother hurt, and fighting his way out was crushing and cruel,
The high of that battle won I can't convey, a silent unwritten rule
Pulling a soul under the door, forces opposing, my body a theatre of war.
At dawn they surrendered, as lightning struck the nearby church spire,
Lit the Royal Town of Windsor and its newborn country squire.

Now I can see how prescient were his rhymes
About the future that lay ahead for the boy who was his mirror,
So similar in spirit as though he lingers here.
Never enough years when a child's in your life.
As sad for the son as it is for the wife.

He wrote '*darkest deep brown eyes I've seen, angel came into my dream*
Sweetest innocence and free, God has given you the key'
Which became a family heirloom handed down
By our mystical prince with the invisible crown.

The father, filled with bliss by a boy,
Gave us his love but left with our joy,
It vanished in a swish as he departed the room.
In his place he left something, just for us two:
A currency those with loss receive,
A form of barter, of value as long as you grieve.

Given once, free to spend, meant to last as long as we pretend
To be living out these happy days, like coins in a meter allowing us to stay.
Traded with the greatest care, to soothe the times we cannot bear
The feeling of emptiness or missing-ness, of wanting your morning sigh,
The brush of your fingers as you pass,
Arm waving from across the lawn,

The smoke of incense leading me near,
Jumping out of nowhere to help me overcome my fear,
Then a laughing embrace because I was scared,
Holding hands walking back to get dinner prepared.

12-strings ringing over sparks of the fire,
A hint of burning toast and footsteps up the stairs,
Butter dripping on my pillow because you wanted to share
All the little things that made being together, being together.

That is what I miss in a day, not just someone, you. The one and only you.

Your lyrics turned predictions. I hear them ring true,
Now I'll speak his honours, before I'm gone, or it's overdue.
A young man was brave to witness your death
The three of us inhaled the same air one more breath.

Today he played me a song of his own
As deserving as any of yours I have known.
Message and music pleading and longing,
Expressing the dilemma about attachment that binds,
Ignorance that imprisons, illusion that blinds.

What better way to prove you were here
Than a son with your gait and a stranger to fear
Like you, to be worthy of his leap at the end
That you may touch fingers or grasp hands once again.
In a wishful dimension and imaginary space
As a final delight, you can gaze on his face.

And I, one more meeting, I've written the scene
Where I get off my chest that one final thing
That I remember when a snowflake spins in the air,
Brushes my cheek then melts in my hair.

The Darkest deep brown eyes I've ~~ever~~ seen
~~there~~ came into my dream
~~An~~ Angel ~~resting~~ ~~stop and so serene~~

Sweetest Innocense. (Inner Sense). ~~....~~ And free

VIII

WITHOUT HUMMINGBIRDS

Without hummingbirds, what excuse for staring into space
Pretending I'm not thinking about you?
My hair like a vine curled around your finger as we lay face to face
With that genus extinct would my ringlet be straight?
Will ladybirds still launch from our window
A squadron of dots at winter's end?
As they race each other to freedom, never to be seen again.
With no clouds to make rain because oceans are dry
Will there be enough tears if we all need to cry?
I would gladly give mine so that others can weep
To stop them eroding my dreams as I sleep.

IX

THERE BUT HERE

I sought your warm ankle between the cold sheets,
Daring to stretch to the foot of the bed.
You were nowhere you should be, it filled me with dread.
In sympathy you joined me at the edge of my eye
So I could see you on occasion just over there
In your blue denim jacket with shoulder-length hair,
In a careless attempt at trying to hide,
Coaxing the sunlight to obscure your long stride.
I asked the birch if they'd seen you of late,
Disembodied, but I believe there's a swing in that gate.

We tackled the ruins, planted and ploughed,
When you felt defeated, that deep furrowed brow
Scowled at the algae, ivy, the brambles,
A garden abandoned, playground for vandals.
The rumour said elegance was buried beneath
So we dug down a century and tried to repeat
The whimsy and genius a gentleman called home,
A shallow beginning all on our own.

Sometimes I wonder if you would approve
When the planting's gone wild and I need to be cruel.
Thinking out loud, should I cut down that tree?
It's awfully old and leaning towards me.
A red kite swooped, dropped a feather that wrote,
Delivered your answer, the oracle spoke.

At the dark of the day I head back inside
And still can't make sense of who lives and who dies.
The door is ajar as if someone's been there
Then I remember the lock you wanted repaired.

Before I switch off the jukebox, just one last song:
Push M7 for Otis and watch the vinyl go round,
Fold down in your chair, let go of the day,
Groove to the tempo of Dock of the Bay.

At the base of my spine, undeniable chills,
I feel you so close and say if that's you
I'm bound by this plane and I just can't break through
Then stare at the bubbles in the Wurlitzer door,
Slide in my socks on that same patch of floor
That our late-night dances polished and shined,
Stepping in sync as midnight chimes,
Lean over the gallery on the way to our room,
Hope you finish that song and life can resume.

X

HE
Never Hurt No One

Born in a row of two-up two-down
Arnold Grove Unadopted, on the east side of town
Two boys and one girl, came the young son
A Pisces at midnight who never hurt no one.

Boiled all that water on a log-burning stove
Shared the zinc tub, took turns with the soap.
A mean cockerel out back, pecked and chased,
A family determined to find a new place.

A child in each arm, two sent away
During the blitz, it was safer that way
Young mother with infants under the stairs
Bred ineffable courage, resilience, and dare.

Fear rose as fast as the doodlebugs squealed
Both hopeless and faithful, she could only appeal
To the glow of the Virgin to spare them this night
St Luke's fallen, no peace in sight.

His father changed hats after working all day
Bus driver to warden, always leading the way
To the underground shelter, crowded and dark
The smell of dust rising, lives pulled apart.

Overcoats, fedoras, stoic and hushed
Clutching her coat, small hands reaching up
Lessons in courage, how not to cry
Hide from the monster until another sunrise.

In the Mersey wilderness, his kingdom of ferns
Setting intentions for all that he yearned
Invisible days, a boy free to roam
Pals by your side? No, just me on my own.

Deceived by the dockside named The Three Graces
That looked down on the slave ships, but not at the faces.
A museum and gallery were built on that stain
They tried but they couldn't mask the colour of shame.

Three teenage scruffs on the bus home from school
Shared one obsession, and it wasn't to rule
The airwaves that carried a new kind of explosion
Rumbled the world and stirred up the doldrums.

Scored hand-me-down jackets, changed the lapels
Pegged some old trousers, and slowly raised hell.
Buddy on the Gulf Stream from the west to the east
Little Richard, Gene Vincent from the land of the free.

They learned every chord, figured them out,
Be-Bop-A-Lula, Lucille, Twist and Shout,
Gathered momentum, that never did slow
Till they couldn't contain it, but before the last show

He took a punch for Ringo, a nice shiner to come
It was worth it he said, for him and his drums.
I can see them now, sitting close, side by side
Inside the laughing, saying goodbye.

Our sleep was broken by an old-fashioned ring
That call at an hour you know is bad news
You're dreading to answer but you don't get to choose.
I whispered three times that dear John was dead
We curled up for hours, blankets over our heads.

Paul, brave and kind, hid the shock he endured,
Hoping then realising, there would be no cure
Don't want to tire you, I won't stay long
I saw their lips moving, but only they heard the song.

It's a well-known story, now legend it seems,
To the school that said he'd never be anything.
A Pisces at midnight, his totem the Sun
And in all his days, he never hurt no one.

XI

SHE
34° North

In the City of Angels and borders despised
Neighbours and kin, dark skin and eyes
Unaware what she felt, one day realized
In a pueblo divided, they were on the brown side.

Lemons and roses filled Grandpa's front yard
Eggs from the chickens, and guacamole trees
Two barrels brewing behind a drape in the house
I could peek on tiptoe then someone would shout:

'¡Déjala mijita! Venga aquí.'
I'd run to mi abuela and sit on her knee
And she would give me a cookie shaped like a pig
Or pan de muerto around Halloween.

Hermanos, hermanas, madrinas y niños
Novios, compadres, primos, amigos
Dressed fine on Sundays, singing old songs
Shots of tequila con sal y limón.

One day we packed up the Chevy, moved west to a town
Where names of the girls had exotic new sounds
Candy, Becky, Jerry, Harriet and Chris
Mucho gusto Olivia Trinidad Arias.

They were all cheerleaders and went to the prom
A clique of princesses who all settled down
With boys of school letters, the quarterbacks, the catchers,
All fell to blue eyes and fluttering lashes.

Post-war prosperity rolled on new wheels
Just the sight of the driveways gave us a thrill
A small pink Thunderbird blinding with chrome
Today there's a spaceship a mile from our home.

My husband-to-be came to visit. I tried to explain
Wanted to prepare him, was I ashamed
That we were happy but humble, worked hard for that roof?
He said, it's a mansion compared to my youth.

Often stayed at our parents separated by sea
In one household coffee, the other strong tea
Our mothers miraculously loved the same song
They were both named Louise but only mine lived long.

From 34 degrees to 54 north
Such a gap between us yet there was no force
That could pull us apart in the time meant to be
Nor keep us together as destiny deemed.

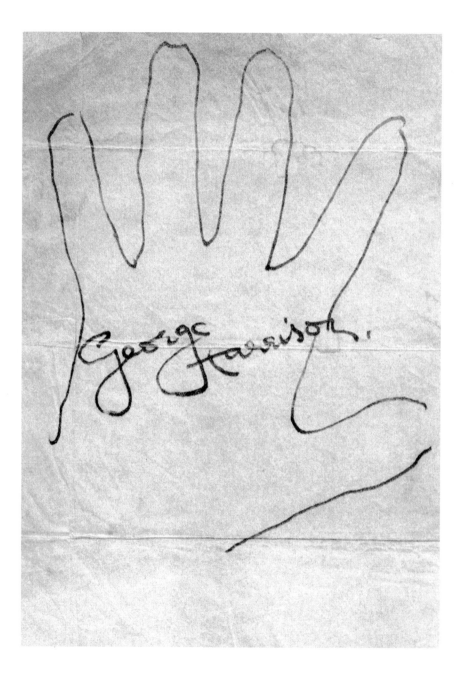

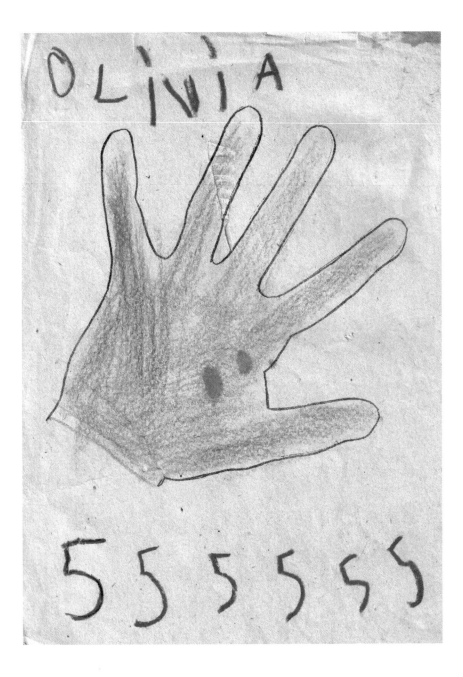

XII

HEROIC COUPLE

On the evening of the century that turned from nines to zeros
We were awakened by the wind of a thousand flinging arrows
And the shattering of glass I knew one day was coming
Bare feet firmly planted, soon they would be running.

Surrendered to repose, tethered by our dreams,
Creating mini fantasies and unfamiliar scenes
The warmth of our cocoon, in peace we took for granted
The pitch of winter's darkness wrote a chapter called The Madman.

On the last day of the year, from across a county line
The loner rode a train, click clack in his mind
Arrived with no permission, brain a spinning top
Stale of cigarettes and fear, sweat and dirty socks.

A round of shards sent flying, by a concrete angel wing
Shooting through the air, piercing everything
The window, stillness, our future, skin,
Faith in mankind, trust in him.

Frozen while adrenalin surged and stung like icy needles
Wearing heightened senses, donned for meeting evil
And so began the play, of some karmic retribution
Or maybe just a random act of one poor man's delusion.

Violence was not our language, we didn't know one phrase
Like charades we acted out, virgins to the play.
A last look out the window, we saw Venus from the bed
The night would end with blood, from limbs and lungs and heads.

That rabid solitaire scaled stone and dewy lawn
Consumed by torments known to hell and other worlds beyond
My hero went to meet him, brave and proud and fool
With courage of a knight and gauntlet for a duel.

I pleaded, please don't go, stay with me and hide
But he tore away and ran to meet who dared to break inside
Walls fortified with goodness, rooms of wood and prayer
All our love and happiness mingling in the air.

Too late to ask forgiveness or kneel before the mantel,
We stood before the altar and blew out every candle
Crushed offerings of reverence once for holy mother
As we ran into the fray of saving one another.

I stood in nearly gossamer, so cruelly unprepared
A naked Boadicea, no cloak or braided hair
Strings around his neck and wrists, tunic made of leather
Two worlds overlapping space, no thoughts or help to gather.

Then a warmth of transformation took my body mind
From diminutive to demon, leaving me behind.
Brahma must once again have stirred the milky sea
Kali floated watchful above a marionette of me.

Sounds we didn't recognise, as air blew from our chests
Not a word was spoken, just screaming thoughts of death.
His bloody handprints stained the silk, I stared in disbelief
Woke to the reality that he was killer, not a thief.

And in that flash I knew, the instant had arrived
To cast away revulsion, aim to kill or die
Apostasy impossible, denied by mind and heart
Yet ringing in my ears, our vow at death to part.

Fear and love propelled the iron, in each and every strike
Without a beat of anger colouring the night
Fortified somehow on behalf of every victim
Mesmerised by how quickly blond hair could turn to crimson.

His pocket versus stainless steel, over and again,
A sharpened tip intended to pierce the heart within.
Six pages of ideas and sketches of an arbour
Folded into quarters as a prescient patch of armour

That stopped the quill from dipping deep into the red
To write a tragic ending, never meant to be the end.
At the dawn of New Year's Eve, walking meadow, field and glade
The man that worked the soil was stronger than the blade.

Demons from a netherworld were surely in that fight
It wasn't just the two of us who struggled for the knife.
It rose and fell so quickly, on either side our sleep
Just a rustle of the pages in the order of all things.

Scars that hold no feeling, it's the memories that last;
Saviours long retreated, hung chimes of broken glass.
Angel wing now in the shed, silk adorning beams
Innocence was laid to rest, too injured to redeem.

The outcome we refused to be, came one auspicious day
With dignity and intention, as if he knew the way.
Death proper, not imposter, by will and not by force
Courageously commanded to settle all his scores.

XIII

GOD DOG

I was floating in the astral
Held aloft by numinous air
Weightless as a goddess in her own supernal spell
Then startled by the ringing of a very familiar bell,
Came the sound of splashing in a haze of misty fog
I tumbled from that realm to my thirsty slurping dog
His name tag met the bowl every lashing of his tongue
Consciousness of God and dog
You always said were one.

Dedicated to Edison, my spirit wolf 2010–2021

XIV

INHERITANCE

You left behind a jungle
Your machete and ripped jeans
Wheels to climb dry riverbeds
The view obscured by orchid trees.

A house below the crater
Where the sun is tied, they say
We hiked its miles of sliding sands
Burnt sienna cinder, trails of lava grey

Naked in the Venus pond
Born of ocean, fire and flames
Elemental fusion
Salty water, Maui rain

A black bamboo basilica
My cathedral in the wind
Where I stand to make confession
Though I can't recall my sins.

In trust you put the garden and a mansion on a hill
A tower I could fall from, if one day I felt inclined
Or descend the spiral staircase
To a cellar full of summer wine.

But of all the prized possessions, only you would think to leave
Billowing white curtains brushing over strings
In front of open windows, strummed by every breeze
Notes to break the silence, inherited by me.

XV

DEATH IS GOOD FOR THE GARDEN

The day of his death, gravity reigned.
Grass at attention to soften my fall,
I grabbed those soldiers with both fists
Threw rocks at the lake and scared all the fish.
Ignored the buds and leaves unfurling,
Snapped bare branches I knew were not dead.
Struck a bird with spikes of a fallen chestnut
Crushed a toadstool underfoot like a cigarette butt,
Until I could not harm another innocent friend.
I felt remorse then blamed sadness, and began my amends…

Found a suitable home in dappled shade
For blue poppies that suffered the glare of the day.
Cut away dieback to borrow the long view.
Gave whimsical shapes to the topiary yews.
I fixed the glasshouse, returned it to glory
With a gate leading nowhere as the end of the story.
Grew Italian sweet peas so they would entwine
Where rampant magenta clematis climbed.
Planted a mardi gras of dahlias and Buddleia Harlequin
To draw Monarchs and bees for flutter and hum,
The soundtrack for a garden with sounds of no one.

Seasons passed, I watched the colour wheel spin,
Communed without, but not yet within.
Each summer I ate what grew from the earth
In September I walked melancholy just as one should.
Chill winter I curled up and burnt all the wood
On the shortest day so I could hide in the dark
Without a calendar to make a new start.

Finally, brave snowdrops cracked frost and freeze
Reviving the faith I had in renewal,
A vacant heart lit by spring, the crown of all jewels.
Bohemian Shades and Tulipa, Queen of the Night,
Primula Candelabra in every colour but white,
Scalloped hedges, a sea monster, tiered plates, sacred mound;
Let doves nest in the chimney, shooed geese Canada bound.
Moved trees like rooks, dried flowers, pressed one type of leaf,
I lost track of time and, finally, I lost track of grief.
Death is good for the garden.

Hi Liu.

3² 十.

XVI

KEEPSAKES

Remember notes tucked under pillows?
A heart carved in a tree
Blue envelope with a foreign stamp
A postcard from across the sea.

Phone calls through the operator
Before our hands grew phones
The ritual of a Sunday
Calling Mom and Dad at home.

A lock of hair, pressed flowers, letters in a box,
A broken string of Tulsi beads, the scent of withering phlox
Through things that held some DNA we felt and stayed attuned
Simple charms passed hand to hand, a ghost of some perfume.

The stirring of the air where you and I once stood
Or maybe just the wind, as I shut the creaky door
Spying elephants of sandalwood
From that stall in Bangalore.

I spread your notes around me
In a circle where I'm safe
Incantations for you to join me
In our secret hiding place.

Your words like echoes conjure
In that deep and nasal voice
With its usual detachment
You say I have no choice

But to let them all disintegrate
Or be found by a curious mind
Who'll write their own love story
About what we left behind.

Celestial Nymph — with the effective encouraging the exploration of alternative life-styles and philosophies in infinite love. It is planned that this will be made available for the world.

october 1974.

XVII

NOVEMBER 29TH

Cruel November, devoid of all but the palest flowers
Taking everything with you, even our final hours
We were wounded and weak, you swept us aside
Like the fiercest wind and the meanest tide.

The shades of autumn were a perfect disguise
Easily fooling my watery eyes.
I tried to appease you with the ultimate price
Offered the holy things, the marigolds, the rice

To satisfy your need and brighten what is left.
The feeling of an ending, a waning moon at best.
With just one day remaining we wandered in your time,
Leaving you to plunder what I thought was mine.

You seize the orchards and drop all the fruit,
Shiver us bare until we feel destitute.
To be as reviled as Spring is revered?
A display of greedy power before the end of the year?
Or just your self-fulfilling name with the negative no
With no V you're just embers, barely a glow.

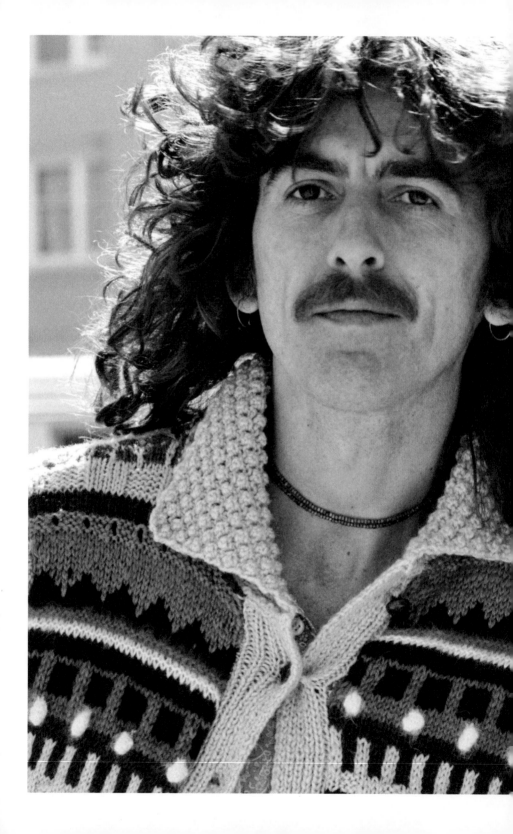

XVIII

CAME THE LIGHTENING,
CAME THE LIGHT

In the three and final days, the world just fell away,
Your essence in its glory wore the thinnest shroud of life,
So sheer it barely covered you, we were not meant to see
The glow of your transcendence, a being nearly free.

Gone was everything you ever thought with nothing to recall
Yesterday of no consequence, tomorrow not at all
Forgiven and absolved, nothing left to fight.
Your time had reached the moment,

Came the lightening, came the light.

We shed all expectations of what we thought would be;
You let go of all you loved, one of them was me.
Our last embrace was reverent, it sweetened our goodbye,
Now mendicant with empty hands, possessing no more ties.

The cloth of life now faded, but love the dye that lasts,
There appeared one more desire, like a late arriving guest;
It quickly stirred our urges, to hold each other tight.
You faced the last temptation,

Came the lightening, came the light.

XIX

CARVED IN STONE

Only the past is carved in stone
So that it will not be forgotten.
This sand, once granite,
Covers and clings to my wet feet.
Ancient geology as I walk to the sea
Each grain a memory being set free
To solidify and be carved again
Marking the time once more
So the past will not be forgotten.

XX

TREE TIME
Ode to Friar Park

How will my life be measured?
By the gaps between my breaths?
In the stillness before each heartbeat
Or the pounding in my chest?

In the time it takes to blink,
By the silence between my thoughts,
In the prayer it takes to fall asleep
Or the loves that I have lost?

Will I see another spring of splendour and renewal?
How many summers will I have to abandon all the rules?
If I could count the autumns would there be more fallen leaves
Than lonely winter hours by the grand hall fire to grieve?

To the velvet lawn we played upon, while wooed by birds in morning song,
To every tree who sheltered us and mourned the gardener gone,
My constant source of comfort, my oldest tallest friends,
Forgive me the cold axe for which I can never make amends.

I moved at human pace, it took me far too long
To understand your rhythm, your timing I got wrong.
The years you stood so gracefully, patient as you climbed
To the sunlight and the heavens, to the tips that marked our lives.

Sure to be survived by the oaks, the beech, the bay,
So many gone before me, do you think they know the day
That I'll be carried down the drive, departing on my own,
Bricks and mortar standing, my form reduced to bones.

No sliding on the frozen lake
Or bursts of hail in May
In the shelter of your raincoat
The mossy bed where we once lay.

A last boat ride through the sapphire cave,
A folly where Edwardians played,
Immersed in subterranean hues,
The underworld in Krishna blue.

Penance, promises we humbly offered,
More so every time we faltered,
Terrestrial beings, bound to fall,
Celestial spirits, in spite of it all.

A final stop at the gloomy glen and the pit for solstice fires,
Where we marvelled at eclipses and awaited meteor showers;
Midsummer night like druids, in our circle made of stones,
In the presence of our shaman, we symbolically atoned.

A rarefied safe haven and refuge from worldliness
In spite of outer opulence, an inner grace expressed.
A lesson in duality, the material and divine,
We indulged in all the obvious, found where to draw the line.

All nature is a temple, formal, wild or bare
I'm at the feet of all creation, for the time that I am here,
Deciding what to plant, to pleasure not myself,
Perhaps I'll be remembered for the beauty that I felt.

No footsteps taken backwards, just the hill that I'll descend,
Townsfolk will tell stories and mourn our era's end,
And say we laboured just for love, in this vale of Chiltern chalk
Where Botanica is exalted and nurtures those who walk

These paths of contemplation, eroded but endowed
With a history of seekers sworn to different vows.
Friars, nuns, agnostics, atheists and swamis,
Buddhist monks and healers, seers, psychics, yogis,

Scoundrels, angels, sweethearts, the ignorant, the sage,
Introverted, famous, recluse or on the stage,
Everyone who enters, faithless or devout,
May leave behind a burden of uncertainty or doubt.

And as I take my leave, I know I'll join that ether
Of all the previous gardeners and loyal staff of keepers
Who lived and toiled within these walls to make this garden fair,
Their wisdom and humility bequeathed to the final heir.

Lastly but not least, how to thank the absent man
Who saved the home of the sleeping friar from a sad and derelict plan.
The enlightened heart who sang to us, simple words in ways profound
The beautiful incarnation now scattered on this ground.

December 2021

Olivia Harrison

George Arias

I have to ask myself, "What qualifications do (you) ^{I}
have to say these things"?
What qualification does anyone have, to be or do
anything!
How did we get into these bodies in the first place?
look out Kid it's 'something' you did.. God knows when ...
but you're doing it again!

George

ACKNOWLEDGEMENTS

To my Mother, whose grace, resilience and example
showed me the way forward,
Mereki & Dhani for positivity and love,
Linda & Olmo con amor eterno.

With deep love and gratitude to all my friends and family,
who have encouraged, consoled and uplifted me over the last
twenty years and during the writing of these poems.
Rick Carter for the first dive,
Rachel Cooper for every step of the way,
Eleo Carson for walking softly.

To the Aegean, whose depths and clarity gave me the solitude
to bring these words to the surface.

To Edison, Stan and Isaac for the silent company.
Rocket for necessary distraction.
Gardeners everywhere.

Special Thanks:

Martin Scorsese

Leslie Boss, David Campbell, Darren Evans, Robin Lane Fox,
Annie Lee, Neil Mohring, Catherine Roylance,
Nick Roylance, Alexandra Rigby-Wild and all at
Genesis Publications, James Scudamore, Steve Tribe,
the Dark Horse & FPHOT teams.

CREDITS

The bell strikes one.
We take no note of time but from its loss
Edward Young

On November 29th 2001, shortly after 1 p.m., George passed away yet the clocks kept ticking. It seemed wrong that time was still passing. The thought of his physical presence becoming more distant with every passing hour, smaller and smaller like a ship heading to the horizon, was too sad to bear.

Here on the shore, twenty years later, my message in a bottle has reached dry land. Words about our life, his death but mostly love and our journey to the end.

Olivia Harrison